A PERIMETER

A perimeter

rob mclennan

VANCOUVER ▼ NEW STAR BOOKS ▼ 2016

NEW STAR BOOKS LTD.
107 — 3477 Commercial Street, Vancouver, BC V5N 4E8   CANADA
1574 Gulf Road, No. 1517, Point Roberts, WA 98281   USA
www.NewStarBooks.com   info@NewStarBooks.com

The publisher acknowledges the financial support of the Canada Council for the
Arts, the Government of Canada through the Canada Book Fund, the British
Columbia Arts Council, and the Province of British Columbia through the Book
Publishing Tax Credit.

Cataloguing information for this book is available from
Library and Archives Canada, www.collectionscanada.gc.ca.

Cover design by Oliver McPartlin
Printed on 100% post-consumer recycled paper
Printed and bound in Canada by Gauvin Press
First published October 2016

for Rose Irene Valentina McLennan,

who arrived just then,

CONTENTS

A PERIMETER

THE ROSE CONCORDANCE

This codex is about identity. I can't help it.

ALICE NOTLEY, *Culture of One*

Wednesday's child is full of *whoa* —

Caught, between ambition and exhaustion,

Articulate —

A lack of blood; here, a yellow light. Here,
a semi-permanent wash of snow. What attention

will no longer allow. Inattention; in

Sleep, a bitter fiction

Babe agape, snores slightly

I am frustrated by the pregnant pause; the snow
covers the basement window.

This is an echo. Winter.

Not the event but language; laundry cycles, sediment.
Nothing settles.

One writes. A lesser accomplishment. Christine wakes
to feed, Christine wakes to feed. I have no reason
to complain. I have no right.

The opposite of sleep is not awake.

Become obsessed. We close our eyes.

She sleeps: a storm,   intermittent —

u((n)in)t(e)rr((u)pte)d) s(l))ee)p

To have everything, but never
simultaneous. Induced, the night
a snowstorm, born
two further days, the centre

of calm. At the time, suspected: she
the daughter of storms,

clearly incorrect.

Write my way out of writing, out
of the house of writing, attempt

to write out a return,

8

When baby spits up supplement, it makes the
formula cows cry,

sleep: her daily nemesis,

Such wonderful scraps. Rose sleeps,
she stirs, she interrupts the poem. I am crafting
a why, when. Rose unfolds, a petal opens.

You are beautiful. You are like we.

ALTA VISTA POEM

I've forgotten all my songs.

MICHELLE DETORIE, *After-Cave*

THE ALTA VISTA POEM

1

shape now the way with hands   , south-bound
, warding further

waves a pair of fingers, arm

such water pressure stretched, out   , east
no loss; we barely noticed,

>   where did
>   green water tower;   false field set with grass

2

construction, layered   camped, in decades
row on row; of clenched fields, words

in swallowed fireworks,
imploding grass; what once was pasture,

>   flock of mortar, sidewalk; eviscerated even-flow

3

breath-glance,   teen staff turn spigot, wading pool tops up
the rules of syntax; disarray,

what shines is confidence, reduced to letter,

CODA: NOTEBOOKS,

in one version, heaven
is a heartland village

you told me once, you told
a thousand times

, wrought iron bars

through all your useless words,

between the stars,
a nightcap

this week a canvas stretched
across old memories

, distorting, distant

conspire to perfect
irrationality

each day with the failure
of a kiss, a promise,

who said, each man an empty box
, inside

or heart, a vacant room

STIMULATING, ROGUES

with nothing else to do,
divides; a conquer,

born of steep; gentle sadness,
machinery

of quickest action

    to do
    what could be,

    done

wave of a hand; unties
to what it holds, suspends

    spending power; seeming
    for its own sake

the worst thing, to believe in nothing,
then to act

MISS CANADA

near Tweed her body rises,
shattering the surface

FALL COLOURS,

Algonquin seasons; pointed geese
and slipshit, park's soft surface

rendered toxic;

      glaciers shift, amid
      the fallen leaves,

whirlwind, drama; compose a song
for mayors-elect, a thorn

upon the rose; Prime Minister
you can simply peel,

bare branches, surface, water
undisturbed,

      not wilderness but wild; bullets
      fly like bees, see pollen, lavender

      , a sprinkle

ten dollars an hour; a turbulence
of shovels, shelves

Tom Thomson dead, no blood
between his bones,

or oil on his fingers, sleeve

THE ALTA VISTA POEM

1

measure, filled   with schoolyard taunts, coos
a spectacle of plover   , sound

    as children, grow   grow older

degrade, degrade,   so sweet, and charming

scaffolding, a bloodless book —

    thumb across topology; a diving bird,

2

is timing, gaunt   dear night, harmonize; on Orchard,
not a single fruit tree   , beckons

; let the spectacle   persist; we deem
conclusions,
    territory, winter; cleaved, an underthought

so fiercely simple; dreamed,   these questions
one precedes,

to close another's eyes;

the former orchard roots the ground a remnant web,

3

suspension sleeps, reflection   and
is driving rather fast,
                                        and
a row of lawns as manicured as time allows,
        a voice of some affection;
scored against a quality of comfort; the diseased ash
        city chainsaws erase, descending
                        and
with no rules; space,
        the airstrip, and its tiger lily progress;

you; and you; and you,

CODA: NOTEBOOKS,

a glimmer; glimpse,
divine

    , a spark

no matter what the score,
of happiness

    , to quantify, impossible

on the surface of this earth
we live apart; together,

if at all;

a tomorrow we once occupied
, no longer

RIGHTS ITSELF, PURE REASON

slips elbows, in another language

    he says, what a disappointment
    this decade's been,

the last eight years; impelled,
secrecy, the dark

super-typhoon to China,
the father of Ulysses

, silent as a cobweb

I want to know as little
as possible; erase her name

from monuments; sun-god
of the single eye,

sleeps, a cold pastoral
not destined to present,

A TRIP AROUND LAKE, SHORE

nothing was required; only smaller
and less interesting

    , rode hobby
    like a horse

flexibility, vagabond; a life of out
and in, narratives

of finding overseas,

    no facts as expected,
    no biography,

water-marks; what words we made,
an imprint

    , salary of sadness,
    cool-minded roadside deer

    in headlights, brush

new windshield's mighty crack,

FOR THE RAIN BETWEEN US, SHEETS

I see nothing new
in the whole of this country; bitter threads

my edge, a pull;

    a larynx & throat-sound
    that you find beautiful, there

    for the life

distract a prelude; you there,
& for good reason,

unhappiness strikes; more often than not,
it has a still heart, there

    & stillborn,

how low the morning, sun
butters your shoulder-lengths,

milk-heavy breasts,

THE ALTA VISTA POEM

1

tense-charged,   streets, run out of sight;
a similar, measure;   straightforward, in relation

clapboard, startle; rare in these parts,

    former cornfields; suffer parked cars;

conclusions, post-war; mid-century, and further; if
in fact a bitter space,

to map and reading, to provide;

2

country made of men,   a cavity
of mighty pine,   staccato;

examine, universe, your conscience; this
a particular and given will,

    swept, sweep, swept,

reportage: roof-leak, halftone, landmarks
low across a deep blue,

    I call you / vertical: look home,

an egg or stone or octave

    3

greenspace   lacks emotion, dogs
confront the squirrels and twigs

on home turf: absolute discretion, just
a fragment, lists

    this blue:
    a song, a sequence, sounded;

walking through a drizzle; plastic bags,

POEM AFTER A LINE OR TWO
BY MELANIE SIEBERT

deepwater smalls, swells
belly-flush, up

in Sarah's eyes; pools,

     a plainsong; angle's error,
     engine of bone

     spent turning, asleep-half,
     change,
        mid-riff, fatigued

sweet cramp, what it carries
, a promise of

     as certain ridge puckers,
     an intake of air,

     is this water to drink,
   is this water to drink,

drink it, darkly, deep

CODA: NOTEBOOKS,

am disappeared & send back
memory,

      copious notes: a postcard,
      yellow stationery,

rarely static;

      an empty vast
      & onwards,

once never thought it natural,

      an intermittent wind
      -up wind,

September rain knocks leaves
straight from the trees,

MISS CANADA (OLYMPIC)

step back, these coloured dots
become a line,

where I am sequence,
bred,

sprint wrap; False Creek
& family homes

pass muster, gold

to embarrass us
back (into) ourselves,

buoyant, five rings
perpendicular,

avoid; downtown
east, side

bridge keeps burning
as I stand upon,

face in a crowd goes missing,
paints,

SEPTEMBER SONG,

drift at night a sleep
of theologian manner,

fled from confidence,
a bore,

    west, is
    unbelieving

con man; could talk
the skin from out your clothes,

    confess,
    an anthem, half unseen

do we know anything? names
of all the ghosts

    in Hamlet;

a character can fathom,
be it modern or normal,

both contain,

    a still
    uncertain house,

THE ALTA VISTA POEM

1

the sudden rain a throat   -song; let
the point of view run

unresolved, a lilac progress;

perennial; infect, infect   can't
help but overlap,

      ruins, further

analogy of green   the dog park, wild
stretch of thought, the fire trucks

skirt figures and resemblances,

    swing low, sparrow, sparrow; lost among the fragments

2

blessed, an hour   , vigor
descend, to incline

, highest point   a sketch of birds,
lone cardinal

      blue wading pool; the line   is not exact,

birding, bottled, bystand; neighbour children,
diving heat,

            so absolute; a tender void in space;

POEM IS DREAMING THAT HER BABY IS A SOFT GREY KITTEN

we know the rooms & basement
empty

when warm weather sets,
I out of words

every blessing looks like someone else

slugger earth & small combine

upon your slow back ruthless a square mile
, fur-short months

short belly of the thing, or
softball without gloves

a photograph resumes

an envelope purrs

POEM AFTER A LINE OR TWO
BY SUSAN HOWE

were we ever that distant; come cover,
translations,

a silent, secret theme

    illuminated
    by every desire, a lower place

a marginal stone heart; the edge
of bird, an empty nest .

    remarkable; analogy of blue,
    moral in a storm

    of alphabet, so baneful
    , starry

behind in each conviction,
certain of nothing, no-one,

HINGE,

a forest of certainty; all night sleeps
the sake of trees

we don't have to mention

thin joint in the hips; replacement,
addled with sunlight, central air

    stay, on the far point
    of water, probability, maple

    the memory a branch,

    every morning my heart sinks,

purple spools from his garden,
just there by the house

    we could mention the earth,
    wrap comforting arms,

THE ALTA VISTA POEM

1

a photo finish;   method, layered
biological adverbs, noun;

what language, reprimands

burning, and the change; instructions, vista
, the highest immaterial, point

     re-working, legends: archive, scraps

I was moving very quickly;

2

winter,   walking, bears   imperfect maps
, a principle chorus

     measured, by the change

a missing house, the lawn
is still maintained; foundation, bare

laid open,   splayed

　　　an abstract bearing: trees, and
　　　tractor-ruts in fields,

　　　3

how long   must I lay, wait
, bird-sound, song
　　　　　　　　absorbed

by ditch and hill, reflecting pavement

describing music, meaning
excised from motion; captured,

　　　fissures: carved out, moss
　　　, diplomacy

A PERIMETER

There is only one order and we do not understand it

JULIE CARR, *Think Tank*

A

The property boundary is handmade (shared). Fluid,
and only fluid. Unless
you know precisely where. The skin

and space of white noise (hearth). One hundred foot of fence.

Language is impermanent. We retain nothing, have no
specific form. The latent grass, explode; infect
the yard and underneath the stone-work.

The neighbour's garden, glistens. Scars. We translate always
from another.

B

Confirm
my personal association. The lawn requires trim,

and so it does.

A sanity short of despair. Lawn ornaments
are temporal. And yet: this sky of relative divergence
upon the written word, my daughter's

childhood memories. What separates us
no more a thickness

than this house brick. At best, let's say.

C

A detail said of something. Beyond the realm
of cable. Naught but ourselves, a once

and future peril. Tug, a skein. The written world
across the line of maples; begin to crystalize,

the thousandth time. Such wonderful scraps, volatile
in the throat. Set, set down. We

can feel it, change. Construction. An impossible sentence.

D

Sleep, alchemical riddle. Dismantled. As
for myself, the sun

has separated out the music. A high
fat content. Unknown beetles
infest the rosebush. Devour leaves, and fill

perennials with holes. A still-gear, noticeably
turns. The south of the church, across

the street. She trolls the water-park on baby legs.

Riddle me this: if one speaks, we
have already been.

E

Why, tabloid, lament? I make my earth,
and hone. Lone space craft hovers near,
transparent. Her playgroup plays,

breaks once for juice-box. Hearth,

we know you by the mess, evolving
family portraits. Speculations. Collaged,

a brick-work. Mezzanine. Intention functions
at the highest pitch.

F

An appendix, to confusion. Property lines, the lie
that ownership of land

bestows. How to claim the earth,
the air? Grease-pencil drawn, a crosscut tile, surrounds

our two-dimensions. Stand within,
and measure. The laws of chance,

and clusters, poach. These patchwork trees, a stretch
of cedar boughs, of hedge. From here, we calculate

a late and arid bloom. A white skin.

G

The poem, sidewalk, collects. To give
me something to be anxious,

anxious. Modes to undermine, the dross
of what the garbage men

can't fail to leave. Rockets, rockets,
rocket; fear they'd set the hedge ablaze. Dolls

abandoned, prone,

extend across the purchase. Oh, yardwork. First-world
this-and-that. Such conflicts.

H

This is what we talk about, when
we talk about. When we interfere, with

a structured, borderless. Such condescending
limits. Do not cross: a courtesy.

A living, being. Polluted. I don't mean,
I mean. I don't mean.

Silence. It could be like that.

I

To understand, such small divisions. The back,
at which we turn. A no-man's land,

surrounding greenspace. Laws,
and those who live within.

Fences, fenced-in. Crying eyes.

The back is full of pain. So indolent,
so full of fear, of graceless hate. The lawn

is starved. And I   can't leave the house.

J

A tryst of confines, edge. The same polluted book.
We are from the future; an impression

of memory

and the haunted house. Birth certificates, waver.
We can't stop time. Consider: earth runs for a moment

in the opposite direction. And who are we,
unless we stir, to follow?

K

We subsidize the path with brickwork.
Hard line on the gates,

a landmark strip. Such thunder,
resonates. Born on the ground, it grows,

strong as an elegy. An anecdote, this burning notion,
cherished. If this is, precisely,

an issue of boundary.

A lattice, clouds theology; renders
everyone mute.

L

Tonal. To the purpose
of a charge, or measure. One hundred foot

of shared fence. This unknown, hiatus,
powdered as an index. Sickness. I will repeat myself

with my step

like earth. Like earth. The day agrees. I am not normally
into sentences.

M

Blockade, blockage, palisade. A model of vigor,
of debate-by-thesaurus. We come from a future world.

Lament: to write a single page,

dear light, the fragile mist. A thunderstorm
knocks out the ability

to advance. What I have left: a gesture.

This fast-acting   remarkable thought.

N

Death, by increments; by small degrees. To
nickel, dime. Of solitude. We stagger, station. Domain,

we question,   who would wish to host?

Hook, and fugue; a hook. Would reproduce,
the classroom copier responds.

The joy at which the heart of, stands
at thirty pages. There, your boundary. This the line

you shall not cross.

O

A constant refusal to behave. Sound, birthed
tomatoes on the vine

accrete with potholes. Never touch the ground.
Such ridiculous brilliance

persists. Unseen insects, turn. A body
still to come. Tremulous, the hand-to-hand precision

of her infant grasp, sage whispers
of the uncut lawn.

Abbreviated histories. A small, forgotten rabbit.

P

A line of black and white. Our daughter,
coaxed slowly into being. Increments. A storm

of panelled doors. Unconvention, specks
the blackbirds miss. Union of motion, imprecision,

and her much-remarked. A signature
of tiny openings. Baby steps. A modesty.

Over time. Less than a year.

Q

Occupy, a purchase. Somersaults
adjacent shared hedge

held in place by driveway: ours, astride
its opposite. A mirror. Conform each shadow,
somehow. Equidistant trees. We step into a measure

made, not born. Facelift, into soil. Bless
them in their sleep. Here, the local ocean

too distant to divine.

R

To magnify: a few surprises, cadence. This
thin stretch of sidewalk, universe.

We picture a river, a belief
held by a country. Mid-season garden maintenance,

of lawns, of morning mist,
of bone. Improvise a scene: precision of

a star-shaped memory, estate   of paneled doors.

Weathering, the best of both. Listen: baby takes

her first step, unassisted.

S

Curtains swell   a (soft) thesis
regarding neighbours. Far and near. What they might know,

or witness. Eyes above, below. I stand outside
construction sites as yards erase; a keep, a castle,

engineered as home-space. Utilized to maximum,
an indoor stretch. Reduced weeding crop and lawn,

the summer sun

reflects heat wake from cobblestone.

T

Screen-capture ancient maps: fringe of farmland,
open source of untouched spoil. Punctuate,

precision. Half-life. Distracted, choral,

anatomy of nothing. Panoramic, a signature
of controlled relation. Hedge, blockade, backstop,

hedge. An outpost, trim. Compass this: a poach
of former scars, lost landmarks. Our decorative
display-yard, from the front step

out to sidewalk. Ministered and nourished,
perennials

line the confine.

U

Birds intermingle, object. A particular incline,
birdfeeder slightly, tilts. Complains,

from highchair to the floor.

Homestead: pioneer, or carpet-bag. Squat, a charge
impossible to measure. Privy.

Cardinal, sparrow, squirrel. The barricades.
Unbarred by field, by speech,

felines stalk the in-between. The intervals.

V

Headway, scratch. A long, coarse curtain. What
had once described our language,

abandoned on a high shelf. Algebraic. North of nothing,
south of nothing else. Strollers, joggers, students

parade past bay windows. Immaterial. Shored up bodies,
no one waves. Without conclusions, buffer.

Garbage truck: a dock, come Monday.

I don't often speak.

W

The compass, names. Distinct. We mandate English, overwrite
with fountain pens, a loaf of bread. Signature,

a revelation. Open facts reduced
in stature. Colonize. Such magnitude of need.

Below, her infant footsteps, pleasure. Staccato laughs at cardinal
and sparrows picking seeds

from swinging feeder. For her, the yard a landmark
of personal safety. The capacity

to contain the length and breadth of her, of us.

X

Marks, the spot. Browned treasure maps, a
copper scroll. She pirates, toddler-speed,

the weight of multiple talents. Sketched out,
generated dashes engineer a path

to veritable plunder. You are here, are here,
calligraphy of nameless bluffs and pudding-stone,

Canadian shield, a higher water-table. Suburban
shopping malls: where we should meet,

if we are separated. Here.

Y

Pardoned, null. Such anxious hands, an
unlocked door. We barricade. For sale.

The notes of children, dawn
and green. Particulate. The yellow school bus, rattles.

Copyright: the lawn.

Talisman of garden gnome, amid perennials
identified and not. Unnamed.

Deliver us: estate, to asphalt. Wish
to craft the savage wild.

Our moral test is to distinguish.

Z

The story beckons, matters. Home, a house,
a burning deck. Such given foothold; jubilation,

a passage laid in weeks, or years. Renovations: line,
and sinker. Half a city block

from parks, her future school.

Lure, lacunae, air: it does   not stop.
A template: plain text, glacial.

Submit: the geographic peak. Restrict the path,
and disagree with each lost step. Enclosed, a list

of bicycles, joggers, dogs. The question of afar.

Submit: a task of outlines.

ACKNOWLEDGMENTS

Some of these poems have appeared in *eleven eleven* (San Francisco CA), *Jones Av.* (Toronto) and *Spirits* magazines (Indiana University Northwest), and online at *Queen Mob's Teahouse* (UK), as well as in the chapbooks *Miss Canada* (France: Corrupt Press, 2012), *Miss Canada (International)* (Ottawa: Bywords, 2012) and *A perimeter* (Ottawa: Apostrophe Press, 2016). "Poem is dreaming that her baby is a soft grey kitten" is for Amanda Robertson; the title was adapted from her Facebook status update when she (and Wes) were pregnant with their Gwendolyn. Fragments of "The Rose Concordance" appeared on *Open Book: Ontario* and Facebook, as well as part of the self-published "house (warm)" (February 8, 2014), and later, as *The Rose Concordance* (Ottawa: Apostrophe Press, 2015; reprint/reissue, Ottawa: above/ ground press, 2015).

Incredible thanks to Julie Carr, Marcus McCann, Gil McElroy, Phil Hall and Cameron Anstee for generous feedback, commentary and conversation on "A perimeter."

Thanks to editor/publisher Rolf Maurer for his attentiveness, thoughtfulness, generosity and speed. Wow.

Thanks to Christine McNair, for simply being magnificent, generally and specifically, in turns.